MONSTERS

De onda first published in 2007 by Draken Teaterförlag

This translation first published in 2009 by Oberon Books Ltd
521 Caledonian Road, London N7 9RH
Tel: 020 7607 3637 / Fax: 020 7607 3629
e-mail: info@oberonbooks.com
www.oberonbooks.com

A catalogue record for this book is available from the British Library.

ISBN: 978-1-84002-928-4

The stage where this play is performed should be an absolutely neutral room that allows reflection and thought. Imagine a room for devotion of the kind found at many international airports – non-confessional, but obviously intended for prayer and meditation. The child who is murdered in the play is not present on stage, but could be represented by a simple, venerable symbol that is shown respect and reverence throughout the play. This symbol could be anything, but preferably without sentimentalising the age or fate of the victim. Instead, it is intended as a reminder that life exists even when we no longer exist. Throughout the performance, the audience is informed that it is possible to intervene at any time in the events that are related on stage. Such an intervention must never, however, be actively provoked by the actors.

The play was written for four actors, but can be played with both more and fewer actors. The gender of the actors is unimportant. The parts are allocated to the actors during rehearsals. An actor does not have to play the same part every time but can exchange roles with the other actors. Ideally, a member of the audience could be persuaded to take one of the roles. The script should be regarded in the same way as J S Bach's Die Kunst der Fuge, *i.e. as a work without any annotation on how it should be played, and where the movements and parts can be played by a large orchestra or a solo piano. In addition to the characters there are two other parts in the play: the CHORUS LEADER and the CHORUS. The CHORUS LEADER does not have to be the same actor throughout the play. The CHORUS can consist of several actors or one alone.*

Any characterisation of the parts should be avoided. We can never presume to penetrate a course of events such as that shown in this play, and to recreate it. That would be almost perverse. We can only relate it. Naturalistic portrayal is often resorted to as a means of protecting the actors and audience from their own feelings, whereas a narrative can give free range to their feelings.

At the start of the performance, the actors await the audience. The encounter should be so relaxed that it is impossible to distinguish between the audience and the actors.

SCENE 1 – I DON'T KNOW

CHORUS FOR FOUR VOICES:

I don't know
I don't know
I don't know
I don't know

I don't know why you came here
I don't know what you expect from a performance about two
children who kill a third
I don't know what you expect to hear
You probably want to know why

Why did that which soon will happen here already happen?
How could such a thing happen: children killing children,
brutally, ruthlessly, planlessly destructively?
That situation must surely be so different from anything I know
that it would never happen anywhere near me.
Someone must tell me why, so I need never think about it.

I don't know why
I don't know if there is an answer.
Maybe there are many answers.
I don't know what to believe.

I don't know
I don't know
I don't know
I don't know

I don't know if you are prepared to handle what has already
happened and will happen here.
Maybe you are not here to understand.
Maybe you are here to keep that thought at bay.
The thought that something like that could happen – children
killing children.

I don't know what you intend to do about it.

I don't know if you can do anything about it.
I don't know if we can give you any answers.
I don't know if you can give us any answers.

CHORUS LEADER:
I don't know what you expect to experience
now that you've come to the theatre to see two children killing
a third
Do you want to upset yourself with an experience that is
– frightening? disturbing? moving? educational?
Do you think it is useful to watch
the enactment of two children killing a third?
Do you think it might teach you something?
Do you think you can tell your friends:
Last week I went to the theatre and saw
two children killing a third
That it could happen
That it already happened
And you tell your friends:
It was

CHORUS: – frightening? disturbing? moving? educational?

CHORUS LEADER: or just

CHORUS: – silly? neurotic? pretentious? sentimental?

CHORUS LEADER: But I ask you: why should we care
what you think of our performance
about what happens here without you?

What we want to know is:

CHORUS: Are you prepared to be a witness?
If so will you only be a witness?
Or are you prepared to intervene?
Are you prepared to step in and prevent what is about to happen?
Are you prepared to go from being an onlooker
to being someone who acts?

CHORUS LEADER: And if you are prepared to act:
what will your actions be?

SCENE 2 – TWO BOYS

CHORUS LEADER: Two boys – Jon and Robert

CHORUS: Robert and Jon
 Jon and Robert
 Ten years old

CHORUS LEADER: Take a child,
 a mere two-year-old, three in a few months

CHORUS: The child has no name
 It could be anyone
 It could be my child
 It could be your child
 It could be the child we think of
 when we think of a child

CHORUS LEADER: The child is two years old
 and stands waiting for its mum
 in the shopping centre outside a butcher's shop

CHORUS: 'Come, baby, come here,' they say
 The two boys
 Robert and Jon
 Jon and Robert
 Two children
 who, before the day is over
 will have killed another

CHORUS LEADER: And so the child goes with them
 Twenty surveillance cameras in the shopping centre watch it all

CHORUS: There, there, there, there, there, there, there, there, there,
 there, there, there, there, there, there, there, there, there, there,
 there

CHORUS LEADER: We see them everywhere, don't we?
 The blind eyes of CCTV cameras.
 Each one watching us with its solitary eye

– you, me, anyone –
Asking the question of the Cyclops: 'Who are you?'
And getting the answer: 'No one. I am no one.'

CHORUS: The cameras have already seen
    Robert and Jon
    Jon and Robert
    nick a few batteries in one shop,
    steal a small tin of paint in another
    The kind of paint you
    use to paint small model kits
    Robert's elder brother does that sometimes,
    did it once when he was younger
    Robert sat next to him and watched
    And now Robert has stolen a paint tin
    Or was it Jon
    One of them
    One of the two who before the day is over
    will have killed a child
    In a sweet shop they nick some sweets
    The shop owner sees them and shouts at them
    But they just run off
    Run
    Perhaps they laugh
    The cameras watching them
    There, there, there, there
    Out of the twenty surveillance cameras sixteen are working
    With a second's delay an image is transferred to video tape
    There – Jon standing at the sweets counter
    There – stretches out his hand
    There – puts it in his pocket
    There – they run out of the shop
    And then they spot a little child all alone outside another shop
    'Let's get that kid,' says Jon
    Or was it Robert

'Let's get that kid and get him lost.'
But just then the child's mother emerges from the shop
'We were gonna help the kid,' says Robert
Or was it Jon
'We were gonna help the kid find his mum'
And she may smile briefly at them
She may smile, the child's mother
And then the boys walk on through the shopping centre
They've skipped school
Attempts have been made to split them up
Put them in separate classes
But sometimes they seem to spur each other on
Neither of them is particularly good at school
'Come on, let's sag, we'll go round the back,
where they can't see us…'
And so they drift around for the rest of the day
Down by the overgrown reservoir,
By the railway bridge
and sometimes on the embankment
At the shopping centre, in the streets down by the canal,
along the muddy bank
At the shopping centre
In the video store until the shopkeeper gets annoyed and chases
them off
Then back to the shopping centre,
in and out of shops,
pursued by the shopkeepers' eyes:
'They're back again'
'No, they were older, the boys who nicked the radio last week'
'Are you sure?'
'Yes, positive, they were in their teens, teenagers,
I'd recognise them, I've seen them here before'
'I thought it was those two'
'No, it isn't them, but those two have no business to be
here either'

'Those two are up to no good'
All eyes are on them
and still they manage to nick a few batteries,
a paint tin, a small tin, a tin of paint the kind you use for painting
model kits, and also a handful of sweets from the sweet shop
The eyes pursuing them
And the CCTV cameras

CHORUS LEADER: And then they spot another child, on its own
outside the butcher's shop

CHORUS: Just a kid, any kid
It could be my child
It could be your child
It could be the child we think of
when we think of a child

CHORUS LEADER: And the cameras watch as they go up to the boy

CHORUS: Two of the cameras watch it
There…and there

CHORUS LEADER: You know, we've all seen the pictures on TV

CHORUS: It's already happened
It's happening now
It will happen soon
Now, then, soon

CHORUS LEADER: Why didn't you do something?

CHORUS: We just thought it was a couple of kids playing
Brothers taking their baby brother home
A little boy with his big brother and his friend

CHORUS LEADER: Yes, yes, I know
But it's already happened
It's happening now
It will happen soon
So why don't you do something?

SCENE 3 – DO YOU KNOW WHAT TRUTH IS?

In the interrogations with JON and ROBERT, the actors read their lines as if from a police report or an accountant's records – i.e. never a situation in which adults play children! The actors should alternate at being the boys. If possible, further into the performance, a member of the audience should ideally be persuaded to read the boys' lines.

CHORUS LEADER: Jon fidgets with his fingers on the edge of the table throughout the first interrogation. His mother is with him in the room, but the investigator has placed her so she and Jon are unable to touch.

He has told Jon:

'I want to ask you a few questions.

Do you know who I am?'

INVESTIGATOR: Do you know who I am, Jon?

JON: No.

INVESTIGATOR: But you know what I am, don't you?

JON: Yes.

INVESTIGATOR: What am I then?

JON: Policeman.

INVESTIGATOR: Good. Do you know why I want to talk to you?

JON: Don't know… I think so.

INVESTIGATOR: Why do you think I want to talk to you?

JON: About that kid…

INVESTIGATOR: Yes?

JON: That kid that someone took and killed…

INVESTIGATOR: Yes?

JON: I didn't do it. I don't know nothing.

INVESTIGATOR: We won't talk about that now. First, I want to talk about something else.

JON: Oh?

Pause.

CHORUS LEADER: And the interrogation room goes quiet for a moment.
A radiator whispers.
Jon's mother's breathing is shallow and slightly irregular,
as though she is struggling to keep calm.
she does not know what has happened,
she doesn't know what to believe.
The investigator holding the interview is restraining his questions.
'Do you know what truth is?'

INVESTIGATOR: Do you know what truth is, Jon?

JON: Yes.

INVESTIGATOR: Tell me what truth is.

JON: That you've done something, and it's true.

INVESTIGATOR: And if you lie about something you've done?

JON: I don't know.

INVESTIGATOR: What does it mean to lie?

JON: I don't know.

INVESTIGATOR: Is it wrong to lie?

JON: Yes.

INVESTIGATOR: And if I say your face is green and your hair is pink, is that a lie?

JON: Yes.

INVESTIGATOR: So you know what a lie is?

JON: Yes.

SCENE 4 – DO YOU KNOW WHY YOU ARE HERE?

CHORUS LEADER: At the first interviews Robert's mother is present.
  The investigator asks:
  'Do you know why you are here?'
  Robert does not know what to say.
  He does not know what is expected of him.
  The investigator repeats:
  'Robert, you know why you're here?'

INVESTIGATOR: Robert, you know why you're here?

ROBERT: I think so.

INVESTIGATOR: Why are you here?

ROBERT: Because you think I took him, that boy, that kid...

INVESTIGATOR: And did you?

ROBERT: No, I didn't.

INVESTIGATOR: But you were there, at the mall.

ROBERT: Yeah, I saw him, but I didn't take him.

INVESTIGATOR: How was he dressed?

ROBERT: He had a blue jacket.

INVESTIGATOR: Would you recognise that jacket again?

ROBERT: Yeah, maybe...but I didn't take him.

INVESTIGATOR: Okay. What do you do during the day?

ROBERT: I don't know.

INVESTIGATOR: Do you like football?

ROBERT: Yeah. I guess.

INVESTIGATOR: Do you support a team?

ROBERT: Yes.

INVESTIGATOR: Do you go to their matches?

ROBERT: No.

INVESTIGATOR: Do you watch them on TV?

ROBERT: No.

INVESTIGATOR: Do you watch football at all?

ROBERT: No.

INVESTIGATOR: So what hobbies do you have?

ROBERT: (*Laughs.*) I sag school.

CHORUS LEADER: Robert laughs.
    The tension subsides momentarily.
    It is as though, for a moment
    what has happened has no longer happened.
    'So, what's your hobby?' the investigator asks.
    Robert replies: 'I sag school.'
    And then Robert laughs and then the investigator laughs.
    'That's not a hobby,' says the investigator.

INVESTIGATOR: (*Laughs.*) That's not a hobby, that's a profession.

ROBERT: Yeah.

INVESTIGATOR: When somebody does it as well as you do.

CHORUS LEADER: And then that little space of stillness
    closes. Robert says: 'I don't know.'

ROBERT: (*Serious again.*) I don't know. I don't have a hobby.

SCENE 5 – CHORUS INTERLUDE

CHORUS LEADER: Wait. Hold it.
>   Don't let what's already happened happen already.
>   Let them sleep for a few more hours,
>   let there be night.

CHORUS:
>   Night colours the houses deep blue, grey-black.
>   Darkness fingerpaints the dreams of the sleepers.
>   They lie in rooms full of breathing,
>   turning in their sleep, rocking back and forth,
>   someone sleeps with staring eyes,
>   someone lies awake with eyes closed.
>   The houses have closed their faces against the street
>   and the paving stones tuck the blanket round the earth
>   so the world is nice and warm.
>   There's the playground in the dawn,
>   swathed in veils of fog and chilly birdsong.
>   By the slumbering bench a scarf and a tin of blue paint,
>   a boy sleeping in a doorway
>   because his mother never came home
>   from the pub,
>   a satchel with torn books,
>   a condom pierced by a pencil nib,
>   the foil wrapper from a bar of chocolate
>   stolen from the corner shop by the bus stop
>   A bike tossed to the ground by the phone booth:
>   the back wheel spins, it has been spinning all night
>   as if on an endless outing among the stars.
>   On the wood fence along Winter Street someone has sprayed:
>   *I come from the future and it's already over*

SCENE 6 – I WANTED SOMETHING ELSE SOMEWHERE ELSE

CHORUS LEADER: Robert's mother is sitting with him in the
interrogation room, but not close enough to touch him.

ROBERT'S MOTHER: I don't know what I saw in Bobby.
I guess I knew that the sooner I got married,
The sooner I could leave home.
I was sixteen when Bobby asked dad if he could marry me.
Dad said: 'Then you bloody well have to support her from
now on,
now, go on home with you, get lost.'
and then he chased me through the house
because he thought I was pregnant.
I wasn't pregnant.
I just wanted to leave home.
I wanted something else somewhere else.
Anything, really.
Anything.

Once, when I was sitting on the steps
of that house where there's a nursing home
dad came and dragged me home.
'Look at the trees,' he said.
'Look at the trees. Look at the houses, windows, doors, paving
stones.
Look carefully, because when we get home I'm going to kill you
so you're never going to see all this again.'
He used his old army belt,
the one with the big buckle.
He never beat my sisters and brothers.
As far as I remember.

I wore a white wedding dress.
The marriage certificate got lost after a week.
I wanted to have two boys and a girl.
So the boys could look after her, I reckoned,

like nobody had looked after me.
We lived with Bobby's mum
When I had our first baby, David.
In nine years I had five kids
– David, Peter, Ian, Philip and then Robert.
Bobby used to stare at them and say:
'Look me in the eye. Look me in the eye.
Do you see the monster in there?
Beware of the monster.'
No girl.
I kept thinking the next one would be a girl.
No girl.
Robert got a younger brother after a few years.
Robert liked him.
They used to share a bed and sucked their thumbs.
I mean, they sucked each other's thumbs.
sometimes they sucked their own thumbs,
but mostly they sucked each other's.
Robert sucked his baby brother's thumb
And the baby sucked Robert's.

When Philip was newborn, I took an overdose of Valium.
It's not like I planned it. I just couldn't cope.
I couldn't cope in any other way.
We had a few good years, when Bobby and the boys
would go fishing a week or so in the summer.
First we camped in a tent,
then we had an old caravan that we had nearly done up
when it was stolen,
then we stayed in a tent again,
they liked fishing, Bobby and the boys,
they could stand for hours on the river,
not talking, just standing there,
and then...

Then Bobby met Barbara.

Her ex-boyfriend came looking for her with a great big army
knife.
He said this was the fifth family she was wrecking.
I told him to put the knife away.
Bobby kept coming and going for a couple of months.
Slept on the couch and followed me wherever I went.
When he finally stayed away for a whole night
I got up and ironed all his clothes.
When he came home I told him
that he could pack his things and leave.
He left on a Sunday,
the following Saturday I visited my parents with the boys
and when we got home the house was on fire.
There was something wrong with the wiring, they said.
An electric wire. But Bobby was an electrician.
So we had to stay in a hostel.

The first weeks I couldn't remember anything about the fire,
I hardly even knew my own name.
Then one day I washed my hair,
changed into clean clothes,
looked myself in the mirror
and I was back.
But not without alcohol.
It took four months for us to find somewhere to live.
A flat not far from where we lived before,
the smell from the burned furniture,
the blankets, beds, the food in the fridge,
everything the fire had consumed…
Peter couldn't stand the new flat,
or us, his brothers, me…
I don't know.
He moved in with his gran.
A week later the welfare office came.
They lined up my boys and got them to undress.

'You won't find the slightest mark on them…' I said.
'The slightest mark on my boys…'

I got asthma.
They said it was psychological.
Like it wasn't for real.
But it didn't get better despite all the medicine.
Then they found a lump in my lung and thought it was cancer
but it turned out to be fatty tissue.

One evening a whole crowd came and visited me.
Just walked into my room and stood round me.
I didn't recognise any of them,
just mute faces, strangers,
staring and staring and staring
and I decided I had to stop
taking Valium and Librium
with drink.
They didn't come back after that.
So I was left alone.
I was never drunk.
I can't remember ever being drunk.
I was sober and I drank myself even more sober.

The older boys took care of the younger ones.
Of course I realised Philip was sniffing and trying drugs.
One day there was a fire in a derelict building.
Someone said it was
Philip and his mates who had started it.
When the police came to get him I said:
'Philip would never set fire to anything.
You're always blaming my kids for everything.
You would never do a thing like that, Philip?'
Then Philip looked at me and said,
'I was there, mum. I was there. I set fire to the house.'
So then I burned all Philip's clothes except for his school uniform.

I thought then he would have nowhere to go except for school.
He couldn't get away.
But he escaped through a window
and stole the woman next door's track suit that was hanging out
to dry.
In the end they took him in.

Ian was bright. He liked school.
One of his teachers said Ian was the brightest pupil he had ever
had.
But he got expelled
for threatening to hit a teacher with a chair in an argument.
Then I met…
well, a man, in a caff…
well, I know his name, but it doesn't matter…
He stayed until I'd given birth to his child,
a boy
– that kid was also a boy,
no girls –
and then he left.
I was teetotal then.
I haven't had a drink since my youngest was born.
I never drink now.
I'm sober now.

But Ian disappeared.
He arranged a foster home all by himself.
Robert went to see him there a few times.
Robert liked Ian.
Once when he went to see Ian he brought
a pair of blinking lightbulbs
connected by wires to a battery.
A green light and a red.
Robert told Ian that they were the eyes of a troll doll.
He'd taken them out of the head of one of those dolls like a troll.
A troll doll.

Robert collects those dolls, troll dolls.
I don't know how many he has.
I guess he gets them by shop-lifting.
This one, he said, he'd pinched in the toy shop in the mall.
He'd stolen it just to get at the blinking eyes.
He was always doing things like that,
taking things to pieces carefully with a knife and a screwdriver,
just to get at what was inside.
Like those eyes.
Like those blinking eyes
inside a doll that looked like a troll.

SCENE 7 – CAMERAS DON'T LIE

CHORUS LEADER: Robert's mother is sitting with him in the interrogation room, but not close enough to touch him.

INVESTIGATOR: You've seen the pictures on TV showing that kid and the two boys who took him, haven't you?

ROBERT: Yes.

INVESTIGATOR: The police have been searching for them, haven't they?

ROBERT: Yes.

INVESTIGATOR: They are wanted by the police.

ROBERT: What do you mean wanted?

INVESTIGATOR: The police are looking for them. The police want them to come forward and tell us what they have done.

ROBERT: Yes.

INVESTIGATOR: Those pictures taken by the small cameras in the ceiling of the mall, they show the little boy together with two older boys. Do you know who those boys are?

ROBERT: Yeah, it isn't me, because I didn't take that kid.

INVESTIGATOR: Now think carefully. Because you know cameras don't lie.

ROBERT: I know.

INVESTIGATOR: There's a boy in the picture with a jacket like yours.

ROBERT: There are many jackets the same as mine.

INVESTIGATOR: But you were there?

ROBERT: I didn't take the kid.

INVESTIGATOR: You were there, weren't you?

ROBERT: Yes, I told you. We just walked with him a little. His mum…

Pause.

CHORUS LEADER: And the boy goes quiet.
  But there is nothing silence can do to save him.
  He takes a deep breath,
  as if he were about to say something.
  But he doesn't know what to say.

INVESTIGATOR: Yes?

ROBERT: We just walked a bit. I wasn't the one holding him. It was Jon who held his hand. I told him to take him back.

INVESTIGATOR: You told Jon to go back?

Pause.

CHORUS LEADER: The boy resorts to silence again.
  But silence just looks at him, waiting, admonishing.
  And then the boy begins to cry. He is crying now.

INVESTIGATOR: Why are you crying?

ROBERT: I get all the blame.

INVESTIGATOR: There now, there now…

INVESTIGATOR 2: We're not blaming you, we just want to know…

ROBERT: Yeah…

INVESTIGATOR: We want to know the truth.

ROBERT: You always put the blame on us.

INVESTIGATOR: Listen to me.

INVESTIGATOR 2: Calm down.

INVESTIGATOR: How are you? How do you feel?

SCENE 8 – AND HE GAVE ME SUCH A LOOK

INVESTIGATOR: Once, when he cried, I tried to put my arm around
    him, to calm him down a bit. And he gave me such a look,
    flinched like he thought I was going to hurt him. But it wasn't
    like he was peculiar or acted strange, it was more like I was a
    total riddle to him. He couldn't understand that I just wanted to
    comfort him. He looked at me with surprise, as though he simply
    could not understand what I was doing.

SCENE 9 – IS THAT THE TRUTH OR ARE YOU LYING?

INVESTIGATOR: Jon.

JON: What?

INVESTIGATOR: Jon, listen to me now.

JON: Yeah?

INVESTIGATOR: Look at me, Jon. I'm the one you're talking to. Don't look at your mum.

CHORUS LEADER: Jon looks at the investigator who's conducting the interrogation.
Jon looks at his mum,
her frightened eyes,
her furious eyes,
her tired eyes,
her baffled eyes.
At the same time he looks into all the eyes that see him,
the frightened, the furious, the tired, the baffled…
All the eyes that followed them when they took the child between them,
from the shopping centre along the streets past the post office
down to the canal where they hurt him the first time,
and onwards along the streets, past shops, doorways,
offices and parking lots.
Thirty-eight people came forth afterwards and said they had seen them. Thirty-eight pairs of eyes.
Some thought it looked like they were playing,
someone had heard the child laugh
as he walked between the older boys and held them by the hand.
All the eyes that see him,
the frightened, the furious, the tired, the baffled…
'Look at me, Jon,' says the investigator.
'I'm the one you're talking to. Don't look at your mum.'

And the eyes follow Jon as he turns his gaze towards the
policeman.
All the eyes,
the frightened, the furious, the tired, the baffled…
'Look at me,' says the investigator.
'Yeah,' says Jon.

INVESTIGATOR: Look at me.

JON: Yeah.

INVESTIGATOR: We've talked about right and wrong and about truth
and lies, haven't we?

JON: Yeah, I know. But I wasn't there, at the mall. I wasn't there.

INVESTIGATOR: Is that the truth, or are you lying now?

JON: Truth.

INVESTIGATOR: You understand, it's important that you tell the truth.

JON: Yeah.

INVESTIGATOR: Robert says you were there together, you and him,
at the shopping centre.

JON: No we weren't.

INVESTIGATOR: Robert says you were there.

JON: Yeah, but we never got a kid. We never got a kid.

INVESTIGATOR: So you were there?

JON'S MUM: Were you at the shopping centre?

JON: Yeah, but we never got a kid, mum. We never never never got
a kid.

JON'S MUM: Why were you lying then? Why the hell are you sitting
there lying?

INVESTIGATOR: I must ask you not to get angry with your son.

JON'S MUM: But he's lying.

JON: We never got a kid, mum. Honest, we never.

INVESTIGATOR: Don't get upset, Jon. It's good that you're talking.

JON: We never got a kid. We never, we never.

INVESTIGATOR: Sit down again.

CHORUS LEADER: Jon stands up and sits down.
He stands up again.
All eyes are on him,
the frightened, the furious, the tired, the baffled...
He has nowhere to go.
There is no place where he is not alone.

JON'S MUM: Sit down!

INVESTIGATOR: We never said you'd taken a kid. We just want you to tell the truth.

JON'S MUM: Why did you lie!?

JON: Because you'd think I'd killed him, that boy.

JON'S MUM: Don't lie. I'm warning you.

JON: I didn't do it.

INVESTIGATOR: There's no point in lying.

JON: I didn't take him.

INVESTIGATOR: Good.

JON: He was just a kid, mum...

JON'S MUM: Now calm down.

JON: If I'd said I was there you'd have though I did it.

SCENE 10 – TV NEWS REPORT

CHORUS LEADER: The boys who found the dead child crowd
together
in front of the blind eye of the TV camera.
They push and shove to get in the picture.
They squeeze in front of each other towards the mute camera lens
They laugh.

BOY 2: When will this be on TV? Tonight?

REPORTER: Just answer the questions. Where did you find the body?

BOY 1: Well, I walked past him first. We heard the dogs and then we
chased after them. Will it be on TV tonight? What time? I mean,
if it's today, what time?

REPORTER: The dogs?

BOY 2: Yeah, we ran after the dogs.

BOY 1: They were barking like bloody mad, and he had lost his
money.

BOY 2: I lost it when we were throwing rocks over by the bridge, I
think. So we went back to look.

BOY 1: But I found it. Here it is, I said.

REPORTER: And when you went back you found...

BOY 2: I found it. It was just a few pennies. Not worth looking for.

BOY 1: I find everything, I said.

BOY 2: And then he found the kid.

BOY 1: One bit first. Thought it was dolls' legs. Or a cat. When I
saw all the stuff that had run out, I thought it was a cat. And
then I thought it was a doll. That someone had laid a doll on the
tracks to frighten the train driver, you know. something like that,
you know.

CHORUS LEADER: And then the reporter interrupts the interview. He tells them to just answer his questions. He asks them not to all talk at the same time. He asks them to try not to laugh. He tells them this is serious.

BOY 1: Of course it's serious. It's the kid that was murdered, isn't it? Couldn't be more serious than that?

CHORUS LEADER: Nearly twenty kids are crowding around them. They're all trying to get into the picture. A girl is wearing Walkman headphones. One boy has a black t-shirt with a grinning scull and 'Iron Maiden' printed on the front. In the field behind them a man is walking his dog. 'Let's try again,' says the reporter. 'Let's try again.'

BOY 2: We'd already walked past once. Without seeing him. When we were chasing after the dogs.

REPORTER: You found him on your way back?

BOY 1: First the legs and…

BOY 2: Yeah, and then the belly and the head, like. Further up the tracks. He'd been cut in half.

BOY 1: First I thought it was a kitten. A bloody kitten that the train had run over. But all that stuff inside, the guts hanging out, a run-over kitten …

BOY 2: Or a doll…

BOY 1: The legs looked like a doll's…

BOY 2: Except it wasn't a kitten.

BOY 1: Nor a doll.

BOY 2: It was that kid they were searching for.

BOY 1: We knew they were searching for a kid.

BOY 2: And we'd found him.

BOY 1: Could've been the train.

BOY 2: Or the dogs…

BOY 1: Yeah, the dogs were barking like mad…

BOY 2: But it was probably the train…

BOY 1: That cut him in half, I mean…

BOY 2: That cut him in half…

REPORTER: How did you feel when you found the boy…

BOY 2: Feel? No, it was… They'd been searching for him.

BOY 1: And we found him. Will this be on TV?

BOY 2: Tonight?

REPORTER: We'll have to do a new take.

BOY 1: Do you want us to tell more?

REPORTER: A new take.

SCENE 11 – I KNOW ALL THOSE TRAINS

CHORUS LEADER: During a break in the interrogation
    Robert fell asleep in one of the restrooms
    while a couple of social workers and a policeman
    sat talking to each other.
    Outside, a train went by down by the flyover.
    Robert woke suddenly and sat up.
    Robert said, 'Did a train just go by?'

ROBERT: Did a train just go by?

CHORUS LEADER: (*To ROBERT.*) Yes.
    (*To you and me.*) And then he said:
    'I know all those trains.'

ROBERT: I know all those trains.

CHORUS LEADER: And then he went back to sleep.

SCENE 12 – NOTHING LIKE THIS HAS EVER HAPPENED BEFORE

CHORUS: I cannot imagine anything worse.
Having your child murdered.
Having my child murdered.
That sorrow is not bearable
Nor is that fury.
That rage.
No one could live with that.
I cannot imagine anything more appalling.

CHORUS LEADER: Or maybe just one thing.
Not that it's worse…

CHORUS: …as if sorrow could have a specific weight
and in that case, who would want to weigh it?

CHORUS LEADER: Or maybe just one thing.
Not that it's worse,
but something equally filled with unfathomable pain,
sorrow, fear…

CHORUS: What?

CHORUS LEADER: That your child is a murderer.
That your child has murdered another child.

CHORUS: No, that just doesn't happen.
That sort of thing doesn't really happen.
That does not exist.
That just happens to others…to monsters.
That's what happens when no one cares.
It's a sign of our time – everything that could be called civilisation
is falling apart.
The collapse of the welfare state.
Violence as entertainment.
Didn't they watch a lot of videos, those kids?
Didn't they hang out in a video store?

Computer games. All those computer games where children learn to kill in the most atrocious manner...

There are no good old values any more, nothing means anything nowadays.

We should be more condemning, less understanding.

The decline of western culture.

Single mothers, absent fathers.

A moral vacuum.

Nothing like this ever happened before.

CHORUS LEADER: But it has happened before.

It will happen again.

SCENE 13 – CHILDREN WHO HAVE MURDERED OTHER CHILDREN

CHORUS: In 1748, a ten-year-old boy killed a five-year-old girl with a knife and a butcher's hook because she had wet the bed.

In 1778, three girls, aged eight, nine and ten,
stabbed a three-year-old with sharpened sticks through the belly, bottom and sexual organs...

In 1854, a ten-year-old girl cut the throat of her aunt's children.

In 1855, a group of nine-year-olds drowned a seven-year-old friend
after assaulting him with rocks and clubs.

In 1861, a two-year-old boy disappeared
while playing in the garden outside his home.
A few days later he was found naked in a brook.
Two eight-year-old boys later admitted that they had taken the boy,
undressed him and pushed him in the water
And hit him with clubs until he perished.
They consistently referred to the child as 'it'.
'We threw it in the water.'
'We hit it with clubs.'

In 1920, a seven-year-old drowned a younger child
because he wanted his toy aeroplane.

In 1947, a pram with an infant disappeared outside a shop.
A nine-year-old later admitted:
'I took the pram outside the shop.
There was a baby in the pram and I threw it in the river.
I just felt like doing it.
I won't do it again.
Promise.
I won't do it again.'

In 1968, a seven-month-old infant was beaten to death.

A pair of earrings had been poked into its eyes.
The prosecutor said that two brothers, three and four,
would have been taken to justice if they had been older.

The same year, two girls, eleven and thirteen, strangled
first a three-year-old boy and then a four-year-old.

In 1973, an eleven-year-old boy accidentally hit a two-year-old
with a rock.
Afraid of what the parents and other adults would say,
he drowned the boy in a puddle.

In 1986, a five-year-old girl took a three-week-old infant from its
pram
and bashed the baby against a wall until it died.

In 1988, a twelve-year-old boy coaxed a two-year-old girl from a
playground.
Seventeen adults witnessed the 40-minute episode,
when the boy took the girl, when they walked down the railway
siding
where the boy finally suffocated the girl
by pressing her face to the ground.

CHORUS LEADER: That's enough.

CHORUS: Wait. There's more.

CHORUS LEADER: No. That's enough.
    We know that it has happened before.
    We know it will happen again.
    But we cannot escape
    that this is happening now.
    Now, recently, soon.
    It is now it is happening.
    Slowly, all eyes begin to see what they have seen.
    The boys in the mall,
    how they lead the kid between them,
    the hood over the kid's head

to hide how they have hurt it

against the stone paving down by the canal.

Now the investigator asks Robert where they got the tin of paint.

He says: 'Which one of you had a tin of paint?'

SCENE 14 – YOU'RE TRYING TO SAY I KILLED HIM

INVESTIGATOR: Robert, which one of you had a tin of paint?

ROBERT: We didn't have no tin of paint.

INVESTIGATOR: We know you had a tin of paint.

ROBERT: No.

INVESTIGATOR: There was paint on your clothes. You were with Jon all the time, weren't you?

ROBERT: Yes.

INVESTIGATOR: Do you know what happens with paint?

ROBERT: It splashes.

INVESTIGATOR: And more…one drop…

ROBERT: You use paint to paint things.

INVESTIGATOR: Tiny, tiny drops, you can't even see them, can splash and…

ROBERT: If you have a magnifying glass.

INVESTIGATOR: Yes, a magnifying glass, or something that makes it even easier to see…

ROBERT: You said something about a magnifying glass…

INVESTIGATOR: Yes, and other instruments. It's possible to identify certain paints, like the paint from that little tin you had that day. You were with Jon the whole time, weren't you?

ROBERT: Yes.

INVESTIGATOR: And Jon had paint on his jacket?

ROBERT: I don't know.

INVESTIGATOR: He did, and you may have got paint on your jacket too. Where did the paint come from?

ROBERT: Mum is redecorating.

INVESTIGATOR: This isn't wall paint. Do you think it might be the same paint we found on the little boy?

ROBERT: I don't know.

INVESTIGATOR: Think carefully.

ROBERT: You're trying to say I killed him. You're trying to make me say I killed him.

CHORUS LEADER: And then Robert cries again.
He has discovered that he is less lonely
when he cries, or…
not less lonely but at least not more,
he is not more lonely when he cries.

CHORUS: At least it's less quiet,
though it doesn't make him less lonely.

SCENE 15 – WHEN WOULD I HAVE TALKED TO HIM?

ROBERT'S FATHER: When would I have talked to him? I wasn't there. I hardly ever see Robert. 'Course, as a dad you think about your children, you don't want them to get into trouble and that... But his mum didn't want me hanging about. I hardly ever saw him, so how could I talk to him? And what would I have said? He was always out when I came by anyway. But if he'd been there, what would I have said? When I did see him everything was fine. There was nothing to say. So we just chatted a bit even if we didn't have much to say. I don't know what I ought to have said to him. 'Hi, this is your dad. I just wanted to have a chat.' He wouldn't have understood. He would have taken off like a rocket. He would have been shit scared.

SCENE 16 – TELL HIM YOU'LL LOVE HIM WHATEVER HE SAYS

JON'S MOTHER: They told us to talk to Jon.
'You're his parents,' they said.
'You have to tell him that you'll love him,
no matter what he has to say.'
That we love him?
How could we stop loving him?
He's our kid.
He's my boy.
He's part of my life.
My love is there even when nobody needs it.
My love isn't a tool.
My love is my love.
Nothing else, nothing more, nothing less.

She strokes her stomach.

Here. Here inside me I bore him. In here.
The last month he would wake me up with his kicking.
'Feel here,' I said to his dad.
'Feel him kicking,
he wants to come out.
He wants to be out here with us.
He wants to taste life.'

When Jon came home with paint all over his jacket
and scratches on his cheek
and said he'd been out with Robert
I went to the police.
'I need your help with Jon now,' I told them.
'He's been playing truant again.
I need your help to get him on the right track.
You have to tell him that if he carries on like this
things are going to get bad.

Show him the detainment cells.
Frighten him so he'll understand.'
So when the police came to collect Jon for questioning
I wasn't the least bit surprised.
'I'm glad you came at last,' I told them.
Of course, they didn't know what I was on about.
'Jon, what did I tell you?' I said,
when he came down the stairs and saw them at the door.
'Didn't I tell you this would happen if you skived off school?'
So I let them in, invited them into the sitting-room.

Jon has occasionally teased his older brother for his speech
impediment,
his cleft palate and difficulties at school
probably meant he got more attention from us.
Jon was just there.
Jon just wanted to be.
He was fine with that.
Of course, he could all of a sudden throw a tantrum,
almost like an allergy attack or something.
I know that a couple of years ago
he attacked that boy at school
and tried to strangle him.
We talked to him about that.
It was awful when they called from school.
'There's been a serious incident,' they said.
I thought: Jon is injured,
he's fallen or somebody has hit him,
he's been run over by a car outside school.
And then they told me.
Jon has injured another pupil.
You just don't know how to handle things like that.
You don't know what to do when someone
who is part of your life
tries to destroy something that is part of someone else's life.

You don't know how to behave when things like that happen.
Everything just breaks down.

When the policemen sat down in the sitting-room that day…
I said to Jon: 'Paint on your jacket, skipping school…
I told you they would come to talk sense into you.'
And then, when the police asked to see the jacket,
just as I realised this was about something else,
something more,
something I didn't understand,
Jon threw himself in my arms
and cried and screamed hysterically.
'Mummy!' he screamed, 'Mummy!
I don't want to go to prison!
I didn't kill that kid!'
I held him close
and I told him 'Calm down,
you're not going to prison.
They don't send children to prison.'
And then I looked at the police inspectors on the settee.
'These officers are only doing their job,' I said.
But then I saw that the policemen, that…
I saw in their faces that…
I could see that…

Silence.

I've tried to tell Jon not to play with Robert.
When Jon and Robert are together stupid things always happen.
Things that shouldn't happen.
None of this should ever have happened.
Somebody should have given us a different life.

SCENE 17 – BECAUSE WE HAVE HIS BODY

INVESTIGATOR: Robert, we were talking about paint…and how you can check where it comes from.

ROBERT: Yeah?

INVESTIGATOR: It's the same with blood.

ROBERT: What?

INVESTIGATOR: You can check where blood comes from too. If the blood on someone's clothes is their own blood or…

ROBERT: Whose?

INVESTIGATOR: …someone else's. Everyone's blood is different. What I mean is that if the little boy was bleeding and we found his blood on Jon's clothes or yours, we would know that you were there when the boy was bleeding.

ROBERT: Yeah, but how would you know it was the boy's blood?

INVESTIGATOR: We would know because we have his body.

ROBERT: Where?

INVESTIGATOR: It doesn't matter.

INVESTIGATOR 2: We have the body, it's somewhere, first it was in hospital and then…

ROBERT: Why?

ROBERT'S MOTHER: To take a blood sample from his arm, just like they did with you.

INVESTIGATOR: That's right.

ROBERT: They took him there to bring him back to life.

ROBERT'S MOTHER: No.

INVESTIGATOR: They can't do that.

ROBERT: No, I heard he was cut in two.

INVESTIGATOR: Where did you hear that? Were you there?

ROBERT: I heard it. Everyone's been saying that.

SCENE 18 – THIRTY-EIGHT PEOPLE

CHORUS: My god! Thirty-eight people!
 One woman saw how the child, already injured, already beaten,
 called for its mummy, down by the canal,
 after the boys had left him there,
 possibly so he would fall in,
 possibly to get totally lost,
 possibly so somebody would find him...
 When she called out, the boys ran back to the child.
 As if they intended to take care of it.
 She thought: 'Those boys will take care of him.'
 And then she walked on.
 One woman on a bus saw one of the boys kick the child.
 She thought to herself, 'Kids nowadays are dreadful.'
 And then the bus drove on.
 Thirty-eight people.
 Some thought they were playing.
 Some say they heard the child laughing.
 Yes, but the others?
 The ones who heard the child calling for its mother?
 One woman told them to take the lost child to the police station.
 'We will,' said Jon.
 Her own child was crying because it was hungry.
 'Good,' she said, and wanted to walk on,
 but she waited, waited...
 She thought, 'I should do something.'
 A woman with a dog stood nearby.
 She asked her if she could help,
 but the woman refused.
 She said her dog
 didn't like children.
 'Promise you'll take him to the police station?'
 she asked.
 'Yes, we promise,' they said. 'We'll take him to the police.'

SCENE 19 – WAIT

CHORUS: Wait. This is when it happens.
This is when the ground opens.
This is when the unfathomable has to be fathomed.
Now. Not then. Not soon. Now.
Wait.

Is there evil?
Are there those who are evil?
Are there evil monsters?

Thirty-eight pairs of eyes that see,
blind as the CCTV cameras in the mall.
Are they the monsters?
Two confused boys who have landed in something
they don't know how to escape,
who just go on, the child crying,
the adult onlookers…
are they the monsters?
You, over there, watching,
not doing anything:
are you one of the monsters?

SCENE 20 – I KILLED THE KID

INVESTIGATOR: Jon, you know you have to tell us everything, and that everything you say must be true, don't you?

JON: Yes.

INVESTIGATOR: A while ago you were talking to your mum and then you asked to talk to me and my colleague. Is that right?

JON: Yes.

INVESTIGATOR: And what did you tell us?

JON: That I killed the kid.

INVESTIGATOR: Good. It was brave of you to tell us. You were very distraught and I was distraught. It's hard for all of us. But now I want you to tell me exactly what you did that day. How you went to the mall, what you did there, what you were thinking when you went there. Start from when you left school.

JON'S MOTHER: No, not one more time. I can't bear to hear it. And when I get up Jon looks at me. 'Mummy,' he says.

JON: Mother.

JON'S MOTHER: But I just can't. I can't stay.

MOTHER leaves.

INVESTIGATOR: We would like at least one parent to be present at the interrogation.

JON'S FATHER steps forward.

JON'S FATHER: I can be here. But I'm not going to listen.

INVESTIGATOR: Can you be here without listening?

JON'S FATHER: I can be here.

As JON continues to speak, his FATHER holds his hands over his ears so he does not have to listen.

INVESTIGATOR: Do you remember when you came up to the railway tracks. You had the little boy with you and... You had walked quite far, hadn't you?

JON: Yes.

INVESTIGATOR: You were tired.

JON: No, not really. He might have been. We weren't tired.

INVESTIGATOR: You dragged the boy up the slope by the tracks and then...

INVESTIGATOR 2: What happened next? Who did what, who held onto whom? Do you understand?

JON: We got up there... When we were in the middle of the bridge Robert threw paint in his face.

INVESTIGATOR 2: What paint was that?

JON: Blue.

INVESTIGATOR 2: One of those tins of paint for models that you nicked in the mall?

JON: Yes.

INVESTIGATOR 2: Why did he throw the paint?

JON: He had...one of those metal sticks and he opened the tin and when the little boy looked he did it.

INVESTIGATOR: Threw the paint?

JON: Yes.

INVESTIGATOR 2: In what eye did he throw the paint?

JON: I don't know. That one.

INVESTIGATOR 2: You mean my left eye.

JON: Yes.

INVESTIGATOR: And then? What did the boy do?

JON: He blubbered.

INVESTIGATOR: Blubbered.

JON: Bawled. Cried.

INVESTIGATOR: It probably hurt, didn't it? It must have stung.

JON: His eyes were open.

INVESTIGATOR: So it would have stung, wouldn't it, if he got paint in his eye? What else did he do?

JON: I don't know. He blubbered. He just stood and blubbered.

INVESTIGATOR: What do you do when you cry?

JON: I don't know. Shout maybe.

INVESTIGATOR: You do? And do you cover your face with your hands maybe?

JON: He did like this.

Makes gestures as if rubbing his eyes.

INVESTIGATOR: Why?

JON: Get the paint out maybe.

INVESTIGATOR: What happened next?

JON: Robert, Robert he… Robert and me, we walked on and Robert said, does it hurt, does your head hurt. We'll put a plaster on it, he said, and then he picked up a brick and threw it in his face.

INVESTIGATOR: And what did the little boy do?

JON: He screamed. Blubbered and screamed.

INVESTIGATOR: Did he fall over?

JON: Yes, he fell over.

INVESTIGATOR: But first he was standing up?

JON: Yes.

INVESTIGATOR: But the brick made him fall?

JON: Yeah, on his bottom.

INVESTIGATOR: Good, what happened next?

JON: He just got up again.

INVESTIGATOR: So he was hit by a brick, fell and then got up again.

JON: Yeah, but I didn't want to, I didn't want to throw any bricks, but Robert said, pick a stone up and throw it, but I just threw it on the ground.

INVESTIGATOR: What stone did you take?

JON: Half a one, the kind they have on building sites. But I missed on purpose.

INVESTIGATOR: And then what happened?

JON: He threw another one.

INVESTIGATOR: Who?

JON: Robert.

INVESTIGATOR: Where did that brick hit?

JON: I don't know. His face. His nose, I think.

INVESTIGATOR: His nose? What did the boy do?

JON: Blood came from his nose, a nose-bleed…

INVESTIGATOR: Did he fall over again?

JON: I… I… I just took small rocks because I didn't want to throw big ones at him.

INVESTIGATOR: Did he fall over again?

JON: No.

INVESTIGATOR: So he got up? Robert threw another brick at his face and he fell over again.

JON: He fell but he kept getting up. He didn't want to stay down. He got up every time.

INVESTIGATOR: What did Robert say when he did that?

JON: He said: 'Lie down, you bloody idiot.'

SCENE 21 – THE MONSTERS

CHORUS: The monsters.
These are the ones you mean, aren't they?
The monsters.
The ones nobody can defeat?
Evil.
That steals on us and can destroy everything,
any time,
everything that has been built up
and can suddenly be smashed.
That which destroys the living,
that is living,
that is life.
Evil. The evil spirits. The monsters.
That's what you meant, isn't it?

CHORUS LEADER: Yes, perhaps that is what evil is.
When we are in a place where there is no love,
then we are the monsters.
When all love has left us.
Maybe that is what evil is.

CHORUS: And yet life goes on even when we are gone.
And love goes on even when we are not loved.

SCENE 22 – FEEL HOW HEAVY IT IS

INVESTIGATOR: And the bar...where did he find that?

JON: It was lying there. On the hill.

INVESTIGATOR: Had you seen one before?

JON: No.

INVESTIGATOR: What was it made of?

JON: Iron.

INVESTIGATOR: How do you know?

JON: It was heavy. Robert said it was heavy. Because I... I picked... I picked it up and it was too heavy for me.

INVESTIGATOR: Why did you pick it up?

JON: He said, feel, feel how heavy it is.

INVESTIGATOR: Robert?

JON: Yes.

INVESTIGATOR: When did he say that?

JON: When he, when he was crying, when the boy was crying.

INVESTIGATOR: He picked up the bar?

JON: Yes.

INVESTIGATOR: He tells you to feel it, before he hits the boy with it.

JON: Before. No, I think it was after.

INVESTIGATOR: So the little boy was still crying.

JON: Yes.

INVESTIGATOR: So after he had been hit with bricks and the iron bar he was still crying.

JON: No, I think he was passed out.

INVESTIGATOR: Where did the iron bar hit him?

JON: His head, on the side.

INVESTIGATOR: You're pointing above your right ear?

JON: Yes, here. And then we threw bricks at him.

INVESTIGATOR: Yes?

JON: And then we ran. We ran away.

INVESTIGATOR: Were there any noises coming from the boy when you ran?

JON: I think so. A little.

INVESTIGATOR: Try to remember.

JON: It sounded… He just…

CHORUS LEADER: He hisses low, gurgles…

JON: That's what it sounded like.

INVESTIGATOR: You said you had killed the boy. Is it Robert you're talking about now? Or are you telling us about yourself?

SCENE 23 – AND THEN?

INVESTIGATOR: Up there on the railway lines, when you dragged him over the tracks, did he lose any of his clothes?

JON: Yeah, his...he pulled his trousers off?

INVESTIGATOR: Robert?

JON: Yes.

INVESTIGATOR: When?

JON: Towards the end, when he was out.

INVESTIGATOR: Did the boy still have his shoes on?

JON: No.

INVESTIGATOR: What happened to his shoes?

JON: I... I took them.

INVESTIGATOR: Why did you take his shoes?

JON: I don't know, I can't remember. It was last week.

INVESTIGATOR: I know it was last week. It's not easy to remember, but if you think of it as a film. Try to see it in front of you and tell me what you see.

JON: I can't see.

INVESTIGATOR: Can you imagine it?

JON: No.

INVESTIGATOR: Try and remember why you took his shoes off.

JON: I don't know, I was cross. I just got cross, and that's what happened.

INVESTIGATOR: And then?

JON: Nothing. Just that he...he took his pants and pulled them over his face, but then he threw them away, and they were all bloody.

SCENE 24 – DOWN THERE

INVESTIGATOR: Did you push and kick him there on the railway tracks?

JON: No, Robert did.

INVESTIGATOR: How?

JON: Down there.

INVESTIGATOR: Where down there?

JON: There.

INVESTIGATOR: You're pointing between your legs now. What's that called? It's not rude, you can say it. What's it called?

JON: Willy.

INVESTIGATOR: Your willy. Everyone calls it willy, don't they?

SCENE 25 – THIS IS WHAT HAPPENED

CHORUS LEADER: This is what happened.

CHORUS: Two boys, two kids
    They could have been your kids
    They could have been my kids
    They could have been kids as we imagine them
    When we imagine kids
    Two boys, two kids
    Have taken a smaller kid
    A small kid
    It could be your kid
    It could be my kid
    It could be the kid we imagine
    When we think of a kid
    Two boys, two kids
    Have taken a smaller kid
    To the railway tracks that run through the city
    – after having abused the boy by the canal:
    They have lifted the boy up and dropped him
    Head first against the paving stones,
    After having dragged him for miles
    Through the city streets: constantly watched by pairs of eyes
    That have seen without intervening –
    And there on the railway siding they have thrown paint in his face,
    Sky-blue paint and some splashed in his eyes
    And he cries: 'I want my mummy.'
    So the boys throw rocks at him,
    Bricks, rocks from the railway siding,
    They kick him and they hit him,
    With rocks, bricks, and an iron bar they found
    They take off his shoes and his trousers

And perhaps something happens then that they don't want to
mention,
Perhaps something happens then that no one wants to hear
Then they hit him with the iron bar
And when they think he is dead they lay
Him across the rails and
Cover his bloody head with bricks.
And then they leave, before the train comes.

SCENE 26 – THE DEAD CHILDREN

The son of one of my friends died of cancer when he was five.
Occasionally, my friend still puts out his hand like this
At hip level, hand cupped, gentle motions,
As though he could still stroke his son's head.
My friend tells me that his dead child is there near him all the time.
He says: 'I still dream about him.
I dream that I dream his dreams.'

My wife and I had been trying to have kids for years,
But it never seemed to happen.
Just a few breathless days when her period was late,
A few hopeful words from doctors after the fertility tests,
A few breaths that seemed to be in time with another life
– and then: nothing.
And then suddenly life took hold,
We saw the heartbeats on the ultrasound screen:
A small throbbing grain of rice.
A life, I thought. A life coming into existence, which already exists.
Three months, and then a miscarriage.
She was my child too, unborn, but mine.
Then we had two boys, they are already at school.
But she – I know she was a girl,
I even gave her a name,
But I won't tell you what it was –
She was also my child.
The whole car shook as I sat that evening outside the hospital and cried.

A colleague's daughter was run over in a parking lot.
Someone who was in a hurry backed out and…
They got divorced six months later.
Their daughter went from one to the other every night.
Back and forth, back and forth.

SCENE 27 – IT WAS MY CHILD THAT DIED

JAMES'S MOTHER: It was my child.
It was my child that died.
It was my boy those boys killed.
When I think of them, those boys…
I didn't know I had that much hate in me.
I am a calm and quiet person.
I've never wanted to hurt anyone,
But now I am burning with hate, fury and fear.
They didn't know his name, those boys,
And my boy was too little to tell them.
They killed somebody they didn't even know the name of.
All he could say was that he wanted
His mummy.
He wanted his mummy.
No one here has mentioned his name yet.
My son, my child, who died.
No one has said what his name was yet.
It's as though he doesn't exist.
But he exists, because he did exist.
My child, now I will say his name.
James.
His name was James.
That's his name
And that's what we called him.
Already a few days after the papers
Had written about what had happened
They gave him the name Jamie.
We never called him Jamie.
We never said anything but James.
As though they even robbed him of his name.
James. The name of my child was James.
It was my child.
It was my child that died.

NIKLAS RÅDSTRÖM

They didn't know his name, those boys,
And my boy was too little to tell them.
All he could say was that he wanted
His mummy.
He wanted his mummy.
And then they battered him to death.

SCENE 28 – MR NOBODY

Before the trial, Jon was examined by a psychologist.
This included a test to determine
the boy's idea of his family structure and relationships.
One of the characters in the test was a Mr Nobody.
Mr Nobody had all the characteristics
that didn't fit any of the others.
Jon gave more characteristics to Mr Nobody
than to any other member of the family.
Nobody excluded Jon.
Nobody disliked him.
Nobody frightened him.
Nobody had mean thoughts about him.
Nobody did.
I was Nobody.

They gave Robert a few dolls
to get him to show
what had happened by the railway tracks.
One doll for himself.
One for Jon.
And one for the baby.

When Robert started playing with the dolls he let his doll
put its arms around the one representing Jon,
as though trying to hold him back.
'That's how it was,' he said.
And then he cried.
'I don't want it to happen again,' he said.
'I tried to hold Jon back, but I couldn't.'
And then he cried.
Then they asked him why there were kick marks
that matched Robert's shoes in the baby's face.
'I don't know,' he said. 'I don't know.'

SCENE 29 – JAMES

CHORUS LEADER: A small kid.

JAMES'S MOTHER: James. His name is James.
    He is my child.

CHORUS: James.
    His name is James.
    He is only two years old.

JAMES'S MOTHER: He was going to be three.

CHORUS LEADER: Is lured away by two boys,
    ten-year-olds.

CHORUS: The boys are nameless
    They could be anyone
    They could be my children
    They could be your children
    They could be the children we think of
    when we think of children

JAMES'S MOTHER: I never knew I had this much hate in me.
    I am a quiet, peaceful person.
    I never wanted to hurt anyone,
    but now I'm burning with hate, rage and fear.

CHORUS LEADER: The boys play truant.
    They hang around the mall,
    shop-lifting, taunting an older man,
    and then they see James.
    'Let's get that kid,'
    says one of the boys.
    'Let's get that kid and get him lost,'
    says the other.

SCENE 30 – WHO IS RESPONSIBLE?

CHORUS: Whose responsibility is this?
Who is to blame?

CHORUS LEADER: The child is no longer in this life.
In the parents' house the silence left behind by the child can be filled by nothing but emptiness, sorrow, rage.
It cannot be aired out, it cannot be cleaned away.
The boys must endure for the rest of their lives that they have killed a child.
Their every movement holds the muscular memory of what they did.

CHORUS: Whose responsibility is this?
Who is to blame?

CHORUS LEADER: Of course someone is responsible for this,
but cannot be tethered to the ground
to be stared at and pilloried
leaving the rest of us to get on with our lives
without asking ourselves if part of this responsibility
is ours in some way.

CHORUS: Ours? What would our responsibility consist of? Is there no one else to blame?

CHORUS LEADER: He who acts is responsible
for the consequences of his actions,
Jon and Robert are guilty of having killed James.
Each and every one who does not act is responsible
for the consequences of their non-action.

CHORUS: How can any of the responsibility be ours?
We weren't even there.

CHORUS LEADER: We are here.
It has also just happened right here.

CHORUS: This was just an enactment.
　　When it happened it was for real.

CHORUS LEADER: Yes, if Jon and Robert had realised that
　　it may never have happened.

CHORUS: But it did happen.
　　So where does the guilt lie?

CHORUS LEADER: We are all guilty of what we did
　　or didn't do.
　　Where there is evil
　　it thrives on indifference, contempt,
　　self-complacency, arrogance…
　　Human beings kill other human beings
　　Children kill another child
　　The conclusion or moral to be found in this
　　cannot undo that it is, was and has been happening

CHORUS: Is, was, has been, happening
　　Is, was, has been, happening

CHORUS LEADER: And it has happened,
　　without any of us being able to prevent it
　　I'm not saying that makes us responsible for this
　　I'm saying it makes this part of our fate.

Afterword

How do we talk about that which has happened, when the thought that it happened, is close to unbearable?

Monsters is based on a series of tragic events beginning on Friday the 12th of February 1993.

Two ten-year-old boys, Jon Venables and Robert Thompson, abducted two-year-old James Bulger from the Strand shopping centre in Bootle, Liverpool. They then abused him and finally murdered him. The photos from the surveillance cameras, depicting the boys abducting the young victim, were published on front pages all over the world. Less than a year later, the then eleven-year-old boys were convicted of murder in an adult court after a trial that attracted unprecedented media attention. They were the youngest convicted murderers in England for over 250 years. Their eight-year sentence was raised to fifteen years six months later by then Home Secretary Michael Howard after a campaign by the *Sun* newspaper. In 1999 the European Court of Human Rights ruled that Jon Venables and Robert Thompson were treated unfairly by the court and Howard's action in raising the minimum served violated the defendants' right for sentencing to be determined by a court. Their sentence was finally overturned by Lord Woolf in 2000. They were granted life-long anonymity and released in 2001. They are now free and live with new identities.

The sources for my work on this play include the interrogation transcripts and court documents from the trial, and a number of books on the subject. To mention a few: *Fatal Innocence* (1994) by David James Smith (also published under the titles *Beyond All Reason* and *The Sleep of Reason*) and *As If* (1997) by Blake Morrison. Gitta Sereny has also written about the case in the afterword to later issues of her book *The Case of Mary Bell* (1995). There are also a number of web sites dedicated to the case and its aftermath.

The idea to try and write a play about this material originated in my discussions with Simon Vagn Jensen, Artistic Director at the Odsherred Theatre in Denmark. We were very hesitant about whether or not it would be possible to portray the events at all – events so deeply and fundamentally shocking. The play therefore also deals with *how* we can talk about that which is unbearable to accept – that there exist actions so destructive in our nature, that we cannot relate them to our understanding of human behaviour: that *children* can kill other children. Can something so unthinkable be told at all? I have two thoughts on the matter which I hope can begin to answer the question.

The first is about ancient Greek theatre. The Greek classics often invoke the inevitable or fatal. Yet they are also about our common experiences and serve to reaffirm our cultural humanity. *Monsters'* structure is influenced by Greek drama as an inevitable series of events, but simultaneously works against this impulse, because it is a play about something that has actually already happened. With its pendulum between distance and proximity, Greek drama gave me the form and the tools to tell this story.

My second thought is a dream: a dream about the theatre. Theatre is unique in that it gathers actors and audiences in the same room. There it establishes an agreement to enter a common fantasy, a common seriousness, and a common play. The theatre becomes the ideal democratic space where fantasy, the flight of thought and the willingness to enter into another person's experience become the bond that links us. Theatre is a meeting place, not a place for competition or consumerism. Perhaps this is why I think that it is only in the theatre, that we can meet one another, to really talk about the unbearable.

Niklas Rådström, 2009